EMOTIONAL INTELLIGENCE

21 EFFECTIVE TIPS TO BOOST YOUR EQ

A Practical Guide To Mastering Emotions, Improving
Social Skills & Fulfilling Relationships For A Happy
And Successful Life

Table of Contents

Introduction... 1

Chapter 1: What are Emotions?........................... 5

The process of thinking in an emotional way
and what it does to the brain............................... 10

How emotions influence our thinking 11

**Chapter 2: The Concept of Emotional
Intelligence** 15

Chapter 3: Is EQ better than IQ?.........................22

Let us examine the major differences
between IQ and EQ... 23

What scientific evidence exists that EQ
is more important than IQ? 24

So do employers now use EQ in
their interview processes?.................................... 27

Chapter 4: Why is EQ so important? 29

Work performance 29

Teamwork 30

Promotion.. 30

Mental Health....................................... 32

Relationships....................................... 36

Conflict resolution 37

Success and Leadership 38

**Chapter 5: 12 Signs of Low
Emotional Intelligence People** **39**

**Chapter 6: Can Emotional Intelligence
be Learned?**... **45**

**Chapter 7: 21 Effective Steps to Increase EQ in
Your Daily Life**...................................... **51**

Conclusion.. **75**

Resources **79**

Introduction

"You will continue to suffer if you have an emotional reaction to everything that is said to you. The power is sitting back and observing things with logic. True power is restraint. If words control you that means everyone else can control you. Breathe and allow things to pass"

Warren Buffett

"Yes, this is true." That was my answer when I first laid my eyes on those thunderous words. It was a message that saved me when I needed it. Let me tell you my story. I was smart enough to graduate with high grades in college. I always had a concept that if you want to live a good life, you must be intelligent. I found a new job and was preparing myself for the interview. I was ready for this job and I was 90% sure I was going to get the job.

The next day when I went for the interview, everything was upside down. I couldn't control my anxiety, so I did badly. The result was that I lost that incredible job. I was frustrated and was asking myself these questions; "**Why did I screw things up**?", '**How could my emotions overcome my intelligence?**" The next day I decided to be optimistic and move on. After that, I got a call from my friend who invited me to her party. I accepted it because I wanted to have some fun.

During the party, I saw one of my old friends and I waved at her, but she didn't wave back. I felt ignored. But I said to myself I would not let this upset me. The party was cool, and I was happy to be there. When I was ready to leave, I met that same girl who ignored me (as I thought). She smiled at me and asked me where I had been because she didn't see me. She was nice and I had misunderstood her. I left the party. While I was driving my car, a man crossed the street talking on his phone. I pressed the brakes of the car at the last moment. I was furious. I shouted and abused him. When I got home, I was in a bad mood. My pleasant day blew up in a second. I sat down silent for a while and looked to myself in the mirror. Then I start talking to myself," **What is going on?**" "**Why are my emotions upside down**?" "**I hate losing my temper**"

In the morning, I was happy. In the afternoon, I was optimistic. At night, I was frustrated…. etc. **"How could anyone make me angry that easily? How could a person or a thing have the power to change my mood in a moment?"** I felt like my life was controlled by emotions. Then I heard an alarm on my phone. It was a post on one of my Facebook groups. When I opened it, it was Warren's quote. I was shocked as if the universe had heard me and sent the solution to my questions by saying **"Hey dude, wake up and control your emotions if you want to live happily before it is too late."**

From here, I started searching for things like "What are emotions? How can I handle it?" and "Which one is more important intelligence or emotions?" This led me to learn about the term "Emotional Intelligence" and read a lot about it because I intended to reach my own peace of mind. I admit it was a little bit difficult to control my feelings at the beginning. I tried different strategies, but I failed. I had ups and downs. I tried others and went through challenges until I found the effective steps which would enhance my emotional intelligence and which also led me here.

Once I discovered what emotional intelligence was all about and how to have it, I thought that it was time to share those thoughts with the world. After all, there must be others like me, who are searching for answers and who are unable to find them. This book is based upon my vast experience of taking control of my life. Believe me, emotional intelligence is a huge part of that. You may think that money can buy you the kind of happiness you believe is what everyone seeks. However, I am here to tell you that without emotional intelligence, that money won't even touch the sides.

This is my journey, but it's worded in such a way that it can be the reader's journey too as the steps toward emotional intelligence can be taken by anyone who has the will to move forward in their lives and wants to see life from a different and new perspective. I did and you can too. However, you do need to understand the process and my research and my own experience can help you. I didn't have that help and when the light dawned on me and I discovered the secret to this kind of inner happiness, I was bursting with joy to share it with others who may, like me, have found themselves lost in the maze of life. If this is you, the book can change your whole way of life as it did mine. That is my hope, that as you turn the pages of the book, you find your own sense of wellbeing and happiness, and are able to experience the joy that comes with that acceptance of self.

Chapter 1

What are Emotions?

Emotions are feelings that come into your mind and that affect how you react to given stimuli. You feel joy when you think of certain things, or you feel disgust at things that fall outside the scope of the acceptable. These are normal reactions that your brain uses to balance your reactions to the things that happen around you. Thus, sadness and all of the emotions you feel are affected by outside influence. They can also be triggered by your reactions to outside influence, so you can't blame the world entirely for the way that you feel. You can, however, blame your reaction to those circumstances and that's something that you have control over. You may not know it yet, but we all do, and emotional intelligence is what makes the difference. Those who do not have emotional intelligence may find themselves experiencing the negativity of emotions such as:

- Anger
- Frustration
- Jealousy
- Rage

But these are not the only negative emotions. Negative emotions are those, which cause a negative reaction within your mind. You may say that you have no control over these, but when you adopt an emotionally intelligent stance, you will find that you have more control than you give yourself credit for because your approach is different. Let's look at the seven basic emotions:

- **Anger**
- **Happiness**
- **Sadness**
- **Fear**
- **Surprise**
- **Contempt**
- **Disgust**

If you look at that list, you will see that more of them are negative than positive and it may surprise you to find that the mind thinks negative thoughts more than it thinks positive ones. So what's going on in the mind when it becomes emotional? Well, you would have to look for scientific proof of what's going on, but to you, you feel overwhelmed by the negativity or can even feel euphoric when you experience the joy of happiness. Why would these different emotions have such a profound effect on the way that you relate to your life? These were all questions that I had about emotions when I was taking the same journey as you are and my findings were rather enlightening.

According to neuroscientist Antonio Damasio, the feelings that we get as humans derive from external influences and he has done much work to try and determine what happens when an emotion is evoked. Damasio explains that we associate feelings with emotions and assume that certain things will happen following experiencing something that evokes a certain emotion. What's actually happening inside the brain is that certain reactions to a stimuli are triggered because the body is going into a response to what we have seen. Thus, it's common that we feel our heartbeat increasing when we are stressed. We may find that blood pressure rises or that we have sweaty palms. That's when we experience feelings such as pain.

So how do we gain better control of the way that external influences make the body react? You have to turn to science to find the answers to that. PET scanning and MRI studies show that different areas of the brain are affected by different emotions and that means that once we know the reactions, we can alter our emotions to help ourselves to remain calm and subjective, rather than simply going with the emotion being felt. Let's take a look at the way the emotion of happiness sparks off activity in different areas of the brain.

Happiness – This affects the right frontal cortex. There are also feelings within the amygdala or center for feelings and the awareness part of the brain in the frontal cortex.

There are a whole load of references which show you the different areas of the brain affected by emotions, but more interesting than that is the work that is being done by the scientific world and the Dalai Lama based upon MRI scans that were done on Buddhist monks. These experiments were done at the New York University and showed that monks were able to control the see-sawing effect of the brain jumping from one emotion to the next or from outside influence to internal influence. Dr. Josipovic, Research Assistant and Adjunct Professor at the New York University stated:

"Meditation research, particularly in the last 10 years or so, has shown to be very promising because it points to an ability of the brain to change and optimize in a way we didn't know previously was possible."

If you need further proof of this link, then watching a video by a neuroscientist may awaken you to the truth about the way that the brain reacts to the world around you and backs up the claims that people who experience compassion and humility in their approach to life tend to find that their emotions are more balanced and easier to live with. Dr. Sarah Lazar makes interesting points based on her experience as a neurosurgeon and upon her own trial at controlling emotions with the use of meditation. In her case, the results were quite amazing, particularly since she was not expecting the results that she got. She found that meditational practice could actually change the shape of part of the brain and that this change brought about peaceful thoughts and the ability to be more compassionate and capable of using emotions to positive effect.

The process of thinking in an emotional way and what it does to the brain

You may think that emotions are just thoughts, but they trigger off certain actions in the brain. For example, an MIT study revealed how there are two areas in the brain that process emotions – these are located within the amygdala area of the brain. Knowing this, experiments were done on mice to watch the activity within the brain during instances when the mice were offered pleasurable reward in the way of sugar cubes. It was certainly proven that negative effects and positive effects caused different reactions in the brain and that the amygdala area of the brain connects to different regions, which are triggered into action by the thought of reward or by negativity. What the scientists said after this experiment was:

"We are exploring the interactions between these different projections, and we think that could be a key to how we so quickly select an appropriate action when we're presented with a stimulus,"

This is also backed up by the idea that the habits that we adopt will also affect the emotional response of the human being to different stimuli. Thus, for one person a very positive stimuli could prove negative to someone else. Therefore, you have to know your own habits and the emotions that are triggered by certain actions within your life before you can control those reactions. Look at the sense of reward, for example. If an emotion leads you to some kind of reward, then you feel good about it. However, if it doesn't, it can lead to negative thoughts and negative consequences. It is important therefore that you note down the feelings or emotions that you experience during the course of a day and watch for differences in your comportment or attitude as these will have been events that are triggered within the amygdala region. In the case of the meditators, these were people who were able to balance the effects and therefore did not feel extreme emotions and were able to feel the bliss of happiness.

How emotions influence our thinking

If you experience a negative emotion, you are likely to analyze it and thus make it larger than it originally was. People who are depressed tend to over analyze and are unable to see any reward at the end of their thinking. However, people who are well balanced and whose lives are considered to be within "norms" can still over-react to a stimuli. As I said in the opening, I got mad at the man crossing the street. In my case, the shock of what was happening that was beyond my control triggered anger, but if you allow outside influences to do that to you, then you are not fully in control of the life that you are living. In fact, you are doing exactly what Warren Buffett suggests and letting people control your life and your response to life. It's like letting go of responsibility and making everyone around you to blame for the way that you feel. In fact, you are the person in the driving seat if you wish to be, and that's the purpose of this book, to bring you to a place where you actually are.

If you have self-esteem problems, these also come from an outside influence in many cases. For example, how many times have people told you that you are inadequate in some way? Your parents may have derided you for your choices. Your friends may not like your sense of style. You may be overweight and measure yourself against society norms, but the point of it all is that it's the way that you see it that matters and if you can adjust your own view of self, you can get over the fact that emotions are now in turmoil and take back control of your own life. The first fact to face is that whatever emotions are doing to you, as an individual, your thoughts and actions are being influenced by them. Thus, the less you expose yourself to negative influences or allow them to become negative, the more likely you are to feel in control of your emotions. It is a case of being in control of the way that you react to any given stimuli. Yes, of course, you will be sad sometimes, but that doesn't have to affect your thought processes if you know how to handle sadness. The best thing about emotional intelligence is that you get to drive the car and that's when life gets really interesting.

Emotions can trigger a spiral of negative thoughts or euphoria to the extreme. However, when you know more about how it all works and are able to harness this power, you find that you are more receptive to the emotions being felt by others and that you are totally in control of your own emotions and they do not trigger so much negativity that you become out of control. Your inner strength will ensure that even when you are met by negative emotions, you will have the ability to cope with them in an emotionally intelligent manner. Think about the last time that you encountered a negative emotion. Someone said something that made you angry. The situation is that you can either judge this as being a passing event or you can do what most people do and blow it up into a huge problem that is larger than life. Most people do the latter, just like I did when someone crossed the road in front of me. By the time you have finished reading this book, you will know how to better deal with the thought processes that follow your emotions, but you will also know how to control those emotions in the first place, by introducing a different set of standards – those that do not judge.

Chapter 2

The Concept of
Emotional Intelligence

We are all aware of people measuring their IQ. This is supposed to measure the intelligence of individuals, but more and more employers are now seeing that without the added content to a character of emotional intelligence, these IQ numbers are relatively meaningless. A good test of both gives a much more balanced picture of who someone is. So who came up with the idea of emotional intelligence? Well, to go back to its roots, you need to look back to the 1990s. That isn't that long ago, but Peter Salovey and John D. Mayer published an article in March 1990, that explains the importance of being able to evaluate emotions in both ourselves and others, in order to have emotional intelligence. So what's different about the skills that emotionally intelligent people have and those that don't? Read on to find out.

It has been suggested for years that emotions rule our motivation to do things. If we feel positive, for example, we have more control over our motivation and are more likely to succeed. However, it goes much deeper than this simple analogy. As the number of people who are stressed increases, one has to question whether their lack of motivation comes from the overwhelming negativity of emotions that subjects feel they have no control over. Salovey and Mayer started their paper by introducing ideas that people accept, i.e., that emotions are our responses to different stimuli which can be put together and represent:

- *Our physiological responses*
- *Our cognitive responses*
- *Our motivational responses*
- *Our experiential responses*

If we know that, then we have to work out what it means to be emotionally intelligent against what it means to have a high IQ. One does not rely upon the other and the paper written by Salovey and Mayer clearly shows this. Thus, someone with a high IQ may not be particularly emotionally intelligent and vice versa. Neither depends on each other. They are separate responses to events that happen in the course of a lifetime. One uses logic to solve problems and the other uses emotional responses to solve problems. You could also relate your thoughts to social intelligence and people who experience this, for example, would be people who are good at managing others. However, social intelligence has also been linked to manipulation and is not, therefore, a good measure against emotional intelligence, which is not only aware of the moves of others, but also of self within that set situation. Emotionally intelligent people are able to perceive things that are not tangible. They are able to perceive other people's emotions accurately and also handle their own emotions in a suitable manner so that everyone gains some form of positivity from this encounter.

There was a rather good diagram in the paper by Salovey and Mayer, which shows the uses to which emotional intelligence can be put. It goes something like this. You start with emotional intelligence and you have a choice of how you use that intelligence. The tree that formed the diagram explains that the levels of emotional intelligence are varied. For example, you may use it for any one of the following:

- Being able to appraise and express emotions
- Being able to regulate emotions in ourselves and others
- Using emotion for the following:
  - *Creative thinking*
  - *Flexible planning*
  - *Redirecting attention where needed*
  - *Or finding motivation*

You can see by this list that this gives an emotionally intelligent person a lot of leverage. Placed in an emotional situation, they will be able to understand their own emotions and be empathetic toward the emotions of someone else. Let's face it, the guy who walked in front of my car that night got as big a shock as I did, but at that time, I was only seeing the picture from a very limited place in my mind. Had I exercised emotional intelligence at that time, I would have been able to use flexibility and redirect my attention to my own situation without having experienced anger.

Something very interesting about the paper on emotions was that it demonstrated that one needed to have a good understanding of emotions in order to handle them and that this extraordinary ability to handle emotions comes from empathy and experiential events. The paper questioned why we need negative emotions, but in reality, unless we experience them and know what they are and what they feel like, how do we derive joy when life shows us the other extreme. A good knowledge of both is necessary in order to be emotionally intelligent.

Presence of mind is another expression that has been used to explain the difference between someone who has emotional intelligence and someone who has not. For example, would you turn up for an interview looking inappropriate? Would you have an idea of the kind of questions you are likely to be asked and by whom? Those who prepare themselves for events that happen in their lives are usually fairly emotionally intelligent, but it goes further than simple preparation. An emotionally intelligent person will know how to impress the interviewers. They are also able to uplift others who may be in a sadder place than they are. They are not afraid of approaching sadness with an empathetic eye and much of their behavior is geared toward making a situation better, rather than looking at it in a negative manner. Emotionally intelligent people are also able to learn from bad situations and use this information to teach them different approaches, which help to swing the balance in favor of the positive. Their flexible approach works and faced with colleagues who are difficult and diverse, an emotionally intelligent person comes up with creative solutions that allow each of those diverse and difficult people to excel in the area of the task at hand that they know will motivate them.

Emotionally intelligent people opt for growth rather than pleasure and can derive pleasure from growth, rather than buying into a commercialized world where people believe that you can buy solutions to your problems.

The way that your emotions affect your thought processes is simple. If you get out of bed in the morning with a negative viewpoint and negative emotions, you are likely to have a worse day than someone who starts the day with optimism and enthusiasm. Emotions that are negative erode the thought processes. They encourage the wrong kind of responses, which is why the number of people suffering from stress in this day and age is increasing. There have been several studies into the effect of emotions and it is worthwhile reading from the links at the end of the book and watching the video suggested earlier in this chapter.

Charles Darwin formed the opinion that emotions were important to human beings and that they helped them in their quest for survival. He was also smart enough to know that emotions are adaptable. Psychologists William James and Carl Lang were of the opinion that emotions didn't cause reactions, but that reactions caused emotions. Thus if you were being chased by a tiger and your heart beat fast, it would be the physiological symptoms that caused the emotions to go into overdrive, rather than fear being the reason why you ran. Conversely, Richard Lazarus believed that the first feeling of initial fear triggered the fight or flight response within the body and that the emotion of fear came first. Both Darwin and James believed that emotions could be betrayed by the study of facial features and expressions, giving light to the origins of what we know today as body language.

Chapter 3

Is EQ better than IQ?

Since EQ is now recognized as important in interviews and is being taken seriously by the working world, is it as important as IQ? Yes, I asked myself this several times during my adventures into discovering how to master my emotions. In fact, an intelligent person uses education to further his career. He has learned the basics and therefore we know that his brain is capable of picking up systems and techniques that are involved in the learning process. However, that doesn't mean that he was going to be good with people and it certainly doesn't imply that he will derive any happiness out of his learning. That's where emotional intelligence comes into play. An emotionally intelligent person will be aware of himself and of the people around him. He won't lose his temper or go off on a tangent when the unexpected happens. Instead, he will use his automatic responses creatively and will come up with creative solutions.

Let us examine the major differences between IQ and EQ

- *IQ is a measurement of a person's ability to acquire knowledge*
- *This ability is something that someone with a high IQ is born with*
- *The IQ measures the ability to deal with mental challenges, as far as this relates to learning new things.*
- *IQ is measured within set parameters*

EQ, on the other hand, is a measurement of someone's ability to accept self and accept others.

- *It is also the ability to work with the emotions of self and the emotions of others.*
- *It is able to come up with creative solutions, rather than standardized ones and is adaptable.*
- *EQ is a measurement that can be improved upon whereas IQ is not.*

You can see from the above that both have their virtues, but that emotional intelligence wins the draw because you are able to increase it by practicing new things and learning to understand the mentality of people around you. You are more likely to feel empathy and also to feel compassion, as well as having a better understanding of self. That's a huge subject that many intellects avoid, preferring to base all of their judgments onset models, rather than being adaptable enough to change views when circumstances call for it.

What scientific evidence exists that EQ is more important than IQ?

New Hampshire psychologists Mayer and Salovey, mentioned earlier in this book, believed that emotional intelligence made a vast difference between performing a task and performing it in an outstanding way. One of the examples used was the difference between building a bridge and creating a landscape by building a beautiful bridge. The engineering folk would argue that if the bridge works, then why does it need to be pleasant to the eye? However, those with emotional intelligence would argue that the bridge should inspire and should fit with the environment into which it is to be placed.

Later work by Goleman, based on the principle that IQ and EQ exist and that EQ is the interaction of the human being with himself and others, the MRI scans that were taken showed levels of activity differed between the brain activity during logical thinking and emotional thinking. We know that the amygdala and frontal lobes of the brain show higher activity when emotional tasks were performed. We also know from the scans done on Buddhist monks that the balance of the two separate parts of the amygdala was more defined and that people who have emotional intelligence tend to suffer less from the effects of stress because they have better control of their emotions and can interact easily with others.

The findings by scientists confirmed that people who are emotionally intelligent are likely to exhibit the following advantages:

- They are more aware of themselves and their behavior toward others
- They are able to manage their emotions and this gave them the ability to bounce back when things went wrong

- They needed little motivation because their positivity gave them the motivation that they needed to be productive

- They are able to handle the emotions of others and be empathetic toward them, as well as being able to be compassionate and more understanding of diverse emotional situations.

- They are able to handle people and use their emotional intelligence to get the best from them in the workplace.

These are all positive traits that come with being emotionally intelligent and my work took me further because I had a need inside me to improve the emotional responses that I made toward the world around me. Anger was perceived as an inappropriate response, although anger can sometimes be beneficial in that it may motivate one to improve or to get things right next time. The negative emotions need to be lessened but also recognized for what they are so that solutions can be found to problems as and when they arise. For example, instead of being angry with the man who crossed the road in front of my car, I would be more careful in my approach toward places where pedestrians were likely to cross. You have to adjust your thinking, rather than letting events take precedence over the way that your mind works.

Similarly, when I saw the girl at the party, as described in the earlier part of the book, I assumed that she was shunning me because I was unable to read her emotions and tune into them. When reading up on this kind of miscommunication, I was interested to know why emotional intelligence enhances your ability to read situations. In fact, it makes you dig deeper than the surface and had I done that in the party situation, I may have had a much more pleasant experience because I would not have let my emotional thoughts rule my negative state of mind and would have been more open and receptive to other people's feelings and body language.

So do employers now use EQ in their interview processes?

OfficeTeam did a survey and asked employers whether they measure EQ at interview stage and if so how they did it. The survey involved 600 human research managers and up to 800 employees and 99 percent said that it was used. For example, the kind of questions an employer would ask would be geared to knowing the EQ from the answers given. Typical questions would outline how an applicant felt about handling failure or mixing with other employees, as well as their emotional comportment in general. Thus, it should be taken relatively seriously in the professional field. The amount of blame placed on others also gives employers a good idea of the applicant's emotional intelligence as someone who is emotionally intelligent would rationalize their failures rather than playing the blame game.

The most important thing to remember which is the reason I wrote this book is that emotional intelligence can be improved with effort, whereas IQ is the same throughout your life. Thus, if you want to increase your chances at success, then emotional intelligence is the way to go. It changes your approach to life. It changes your reactions to other people, it helps you to know your own limitations and to work toward improving any limitation that you feel you may currently have. It's indeed a very painful journey at first, but once you get accustomed to knowing who you are in relationship to the world around you, it increases your chances of success. It was a hard pill for me to swallow, but once I took that route, the changes in my life were amazing. That's why I wanted to get it all down on paper so that you too can experience increasing your EQ and thus increasing the likelihood of success in everything that you do in your life.

Chapter 4

Why is EQ so important?

If you cannot manage your emotions and the emotions of others, your life is disadvantaged in many ways. In this chapter, I will look at those ways so that you get a better understanding of why it's important to increase your EQ level if you want to make the most of your life.

Work performance

You may have a very high IQ, but if you are not a people person, then you are not a great leader. You may have known bosses during the course of your life that will never really go far in their lives because they feel no empathy, have little patience for their staff and really don't know how to work as a team. They are also the people who will gladly take credit for the things that have been achieved by others. Anyone of these traits can follow a person if they have no EQ. They simply don't care about others enough to let them enter the equation. Now, let's look at how EQ changes work performance.

Teamwork

Someone with EQ will know the members of staff and will be aware of their emotional strengths and weaknesses. They will not place the wrong members of the team in positions of vulnerability. Instead, they will place team members where their strengths lie because they will get better results. For example, some people work better independently of others and they would be placed in jobs that allow them that freedom to work alone but within the level of the capability. Others like to be in a team and work well with team members. These are people a manager with a high EQ would place together so that they are able to bring out the best in each other.

Promotion

Over the years, employment has become more and more important. It doesn't matter if you have a glowing resume if you don't have EQ, it is likely that you will be passed over for promotion. The reason isn't your level of activity or even your capability. Where the weakness lies in that you tend to hoard your work, thinking you are the best person to do it. You tend to clear your desk regularly because you think you need to prove that you can go above and beyond what is normal. The problem with this theory is that you are not management material. You don't know how to share your workload or teach others. You don't encourage others to succeed. You don't know how to delegate and will fail as a manager because of all of these faults, even though you may be more qualified on paper and have a higher IQ. Emotional intelligence means that you are better placed for promotion. You know how to handle people and you face the workload with enthusiasm and positivity that drives others.

Your work performance is better because you know how to prioritize. You also know how to handle your time if you have emotional intelligence because you know your own weaknesses and work around them, rather than seeing them as flaws and hiding them. You are able to gauge people better and can enlist help from the right people, thus getting the job done more efficiently. Your success rate will also be high and even if you fail, you will use failures as learning curves rather than become frustrated by them.

When you look at top entrepreneurs like Virgin boss, Richard Branson, you will find that they don't purport to be perfect or to have perfect solutions. They employ good people to do the jobs they need to be done, and Richard has said that he embraces mistakes rather than regrets them because they teach him better ways to do things. That's what EQ does. He is empathetic with his employees and knows their strengths and weaknesses and works toward providing them with a workplace that is dynamic and that feeds their enthusiasm rather than dampening it.

Mental Health

This is a massive subject. Do you know the percentage of people being treated for stress related ailments in the US in one year? There are 43.8 billion human beings who are treated for some kind of mental illness in the United States every single year and the numbers are not going down. The statistics mentioned were gathered on a very reputable website that collates numbers relating to mental health called The National Alliance on Mental Health. I mentioned earlier in the book that scientists and psychologists have even been having meetings with the Dalai Lama in order to find out how systems in use by Buddhists can be used in the general population to help lower these numbers. There are several books following this discourse on Amazon, and they make a very interesting read, particularly from the point of emotional intelligence and mental health issues.

In this day and age, there is so much stress placed on the modern population that they are ill equipped to deal with it. Thus, more and more classes have been introduced in mindfulness and meditation to slow down that process of overthinking things and to be able to provide practitioners with the opportunity to get to know themselves and to feel that they fit into modern society in a more acceptable way. From self-love to gratitude, the feelings that human beings go through in their lives are as a direct result of emotional input. The negativity that you feel comes from emotions. The positivity that you experience also comes from emotions, but the brain is more likely to think in the negative form than the positive one. It's the survival instinct that every human being was born with. The problem with this is that it also makes us skeptical and with so many interferences from this technical age, human beings have forgotten to use things such as instinct or gut feeling because their lives don't give them the time to experience these and they are also influenced by the media and the expected reactions of society in general.

What interested me the most about this kind of solution is that it's there for everyone who chooses to pursue it. It is not exclusive like high IQ is. With training, anyone can experience emotional intelligence and profit from it. In the chapter that deals with solutions and steps to increase your emotional intelligence, you will find that some of these seem basic, but we have lost touch with basics these days and put all of our trust on modern technology to solve problems that are not machine made. These are emotional problems that come to the mind through negative thinking, which is also inherent with the human race. The National Science Foundation published a paper in 2005 and what this showed was that the thoughts that come to your mind take a pattern.

95 percent of your thoughts are repetitive thoughts. This means that they are thoughts that run through your mind during the course of your life and may even be day to day. For example, "I must make the dinner" or "I must switch off the alarm." Everything that

forms the thoughts centered upon tasks that you do are repetitive thoughts. On top of that, they found that 80 percent of your thoughts are negative. These are the "What if…" or "I wish I had…" type of thoughts or the thoughts that critique yourself or others. That's a huge percentage isn't it? So how can you expect yourself to be in control of your mental welfare when the human brain is throwing this many negative thoughts into your life each day? The answer is to learn to harness those thoughts and that's what mindfulness and meditation teach you to do. You may have heard of people using things like affirmations or being asked to replace negative thoughts with positive responses and the reason that this is done is so that the subconscious mind registers the new reaction because it is repeated sufficient times to become a habit that replaces the negative approach.

Mindfulness has been used on mental health patients in the United Kingdom for some time now and is showing great success. If you watched the video that I directed you to earlier by the neuroscientist, you will also have had her confirmation that this simple change in your approach to life helps you to feel happier and more capable of being positive toward others. Mental health relies upon positive input and that doesn't have to be from others. If you rely too much on the approval of others, then you are not looking into your own way of life in an emotionally intelligent manner. You are using others for props and without their validation, you feel that you are not worthy. That's why people are encouraged to learn about themselves and learn to accept self rather than depending upon others for validation that may not happen.

Relationships

There's a lot of give and take with a successful relationship, but it's much more than that. When someone is comfortable in the skin they are in, they offer more to their friendships. They are not needy. They do not rely upon friends for positive input but can create this positive input within themselves. During the course of my life, I have known people who say they "cannot" cope alone. The thing is that everyone can if they have the emotional intelligence to do it. It starts with the thoughts that you have and the emotions with which they are greeted. If you do not have self-love, it's unreasonable to expect love from others. Why would they want someone who is incomplete? To compensate for this, many people use themselves as doormats because it makes them feel validated. She needs me to babysit whenever she wants to go out. He needs me because I have purposely not let him near the kitchen and if I wasn't there, he would starve. Come on, be real. If you are in a relationship that is worth its salt and you are also emotionally intelligent you realize that your life and the life of a partner or lover are two separate things. Each has their own level of personal growth. In an ideal situation with someone who is emotionally intelligent, they will encourage you to learn new things or to be that individual that you are, rather than restraining you in some way. That control that you let others have over who you are shows a decided lack of emotional intelligence, but as I said in a previous chapter, you don't have to stay stuck in that situation, because emotional intelligence can be learned.

Conflict resolution

People with a high level of emotional intelligence are able to adjust situations more easily because they don't look at failure in the same way as those who only have IQ and who may be phased by failure. They look at conflicts from many angles and are able to take all sides into account, rather than seeing the conflict from a myopic viewpoint.

Success and Leadership

Those with a good strong emotional intelligence make better leaders and experience more success because their success is not single-minded. They are able to work well with others and supervise in a better way than those with a high IQ. They are people friendly and that means that they will take into account the personal strengths and weaknesses of others, thus producing a better and quicker result. They lead by example, not by fear and those who work for them are impressed at their ability to adjust to the variety of situations that are presented in a world of constant competition.

These are the reasons why emotional intelligence is much more important than IQ. You determine the level of emotional intelligence by learning how to increase it and make your life so much more than it is now by doing just that.

Chapter 5

12 Signs of Low Emotional Intelligence People

Low emotional intelligence means that people fly off the hand easily because they are not adaptable. It also means that much of the time they are not aware of their emotional entanglement in everyday situations. These are people who may lose their temper easily, and who play the blame game because they don't want to take responsibility for when things go wrong. If you deal with people with low emotional intelligence you are likely to experience the following.

Let's look at some questions that will help you to decide how emotionally intelligent people around you are and how it may affect you.

1. **Does your partner get frustrated and angry at life?** The chances are that he/she is more frustrated with herself or himself because they are not getting the same as you are from the relationship. Beware. It may take a great deal of patience on your part to put things right, including trying to bolster your partner's understanding of emotional intelligence.

2. **Does your boss shout a lot?** – You may find that you are scared of your boss and this isn't a good sign. Not only will people resent working for him, but they will not respect him. Eventually this will make you dread going to work.

3. **Does your boss take the credit for things you did?** – This shows little empathy for his fellow workers. As long as the job is done, he doesn't recognize those who did it. Don't expect positive encouragement because the boss only gives this when he needs something.

4. **Do you suffer from depression?** – The chances are that your emotional intelligence is low if you do and that by increasing it, you can and will make positive changes to your life.

5. **Do you see the cup as half full or half empty?** – The chances are that if you are reading this book you are a little pessimistic toward life and you can change that by using emotional intelligence to up the positivity in your life and start believing in the half full cup.

6. **Do you find yourself anxious when you are not doing something?** – Here, the problem is that you have not yet found peace within yourself. Thus, you are uncomfortable spending time alone and seek out the company of others or activities to hide this trait. Emotional intelligence will help you to get over it.

7. **Do you find it hard to relate to others?** – People with low emotional intelligence do have problems because they are too inward looking. Their expectations of others are too high and not at all compassionate.

8. **Do you depend upon others for validation?** – This is a sign of low emotional intelligence. In fact, you are so reliant upon others that you become a burden to them through constantly seeking approval and validation. Emotional intelligence, in this case, will help you to be less of a burden and more self-sufficient.

9. **Do you find you look back on the past a lot?** – People who do this miss out on what's happening now in their lives. They analyze life rather than living it.

10. **Do you find that you worry about the future?** – Again, people who spend all of their time worrying about the future don't spend much time in the moment they are in, thus losing opportunities to enjoy life to its fullest. Emotional intelligence helps them to be more present in their lives and that makes a huge difference to their perception of life.

11. **Do you find that you are not good in social situations and cannot read people?** – The problem here is that your esteem levels are already too low and thus, you find it hard to relate to others and worry about social

interaction. Emotional intelligence helps you to come to terms with who you are and thus makes it easier to accept all kinds of social interaction.

12. **Do you panic when things go wrong?** – This is the perfect sign that your emotional intelligence needs to be increased. Emotionally intelligent people are able to pick themselves up and find another approach through their experiences and don't tend to look back on mistakes.

Apart from these obvious 12 signs of lack of emotional intelligence, there are others:

- *Lack of forgiveness of others*
- *Lack of forgiveness of self*
- *Lack of acceptance of self*

These can be put under the other headings, but I thought it relevant to mention them because unless you deal with these, you will always allow the above situations to happen to you and thus not display any kind of emotional intelligence because you can't forgive. Thus forgiveness needs to be high on your list of priorities.

If you see any of the above as being something that is relevant to your life, you need not worry. All of them will fade into obscurity once you start to grasp how emotional intelligence works and what it does for you. You may not believe it now, but as you go through the rest of this book, it is hoped that you can work on your emotional intelligence level so that you can cross these off your list of miseries! I did and I know that I was skeptical at first. Now that I have gained the emotional intelligence I once lacked, I decided to write this book to help others in situations that are similar to that which I accepted as the norm. It isn't. You can change it. All you need to do is take a new approach and the chapters that follow will show you how.

Chapter 6

Can Emotional Intelligence be Learned?

It is common that people ask this question and the good news is that while some people have EQ as a natural talent, for those who don't, these skills can be learned. You see, people come from all kinds of backgrounds and these determine to a large extent how they approach their adult lives. You are taught by parents how to approach your life and some parents are more talented at this skill than others, so it follows that some kids with learn emotional intelligence from an early age, while others will find it harder to adjust their lives. You see, when you leave home as an adult, you already have set ideas and ideals in your mind, but life evolves and these change as you start to become an adult in the true sense of the word, making your own decisions. Those who have low emotional intelligence have never been shown how to react to life any differently, but there are different approaches that can increase their potential and it is these that they need to learn and understand in order to do that.

- **Self-awareness**
- **Self-regulation (managing emotions)**
- **Self-motivation**
- **Recognizing other emotions (empathy)**
- **Social skills**

These are the basics of emotional intelligence. So what do they mean in your life and how does emotional intelligence make a difference? In the next chapter you will find detailed information on 21 changes you can make in your life that will help you to increase your emotional intelligence. However, you need to see the benefits of learning before you actually approach doing it, so that you are going into this with your eyes open to the potential of success. This chapter is really written to show you how emotional intelligence applies to each of the above items.

Self-awareness – Do you really know who you are and what you want out of life? Are you happy with who you are? David felt that he wasn't that important in the order of things. He had a high IQ and could do most things, but socially he was inadequate. He thought that the problem lay with others, rather than himself. He was not aware of how others perceived him. He was unaware of his own body language and how awkward he appeared to others and why people were alienated by him. None of this was intentional, but by learning self-awareness, he was able to overcome the difficulties that his past had put in the way of making friends. By becoming aware of himself, he also started to like who he was and he learned that the more positive he felt about himself, the more positive others felt toward him. Self-awareness is where it all starts and to become self-aware, you use a series of exercises, such as meditation, journaling and observation to improve your level of emotional understanding of yourself.

Self-regulation – In this case, you are not emotionally aware of why you lose your temper, why you blame others and why your emotions take control of your approach to life. These emotions needs to be harnessed in some way. In the case of William, he lost his temper on a regular basis. Life seemed to be against him. However, when he talked about his problems much of this stemmed from inner frustration and lack of patience on his part. Through meditation and counseling, he was able to get back on track. You may not need counseling, but if you can learn about the triggers that put you into this state, it puts you in a better position to examine different reactions to those triggers and that's when you start to let emotional intelligence help you to self-regulate.

Self-motivation – Some people use others as crutches for their lives. Polly achieved what she did because she lived off the praise of others, but this isn't a very emotionally intelligent approach to life. Learning about mindfulness, she suddenly realized that what she craved from others could be found within her own mind. The self-motivation was there, but she had not tapped into it because she had not known how to do that. Mindfulness made her more aware that her own assessment of her performance was more relevant than the assessment made by people outside of self. When she learned that, she did it through goal setting and reward. This is a good way to move forward and to use emotional intelligence to achieve. She also learned to understand others and emotional intelligence showed her how others thought, how others reacted to her and indeed it was a shock to learn that she had lacked so much self-motivation that she had been a burden to people around her in her search for approval. Many people do this and get stuck into a vicious circle of needing validation from others to gain the energy to actually self-motivate, but when she learned self-motivation, her life changed considerably for the better.

Recognizing the emotions of others – We are often so filled with our own emotional feelings and thoughts that we don't take account of the feelings of others. We slam our way through life and wonder why other people don't understand us. When Susan took a course in mindfulness, she was shocked at what she found out about herself. All of her life she had placed judgment on people. It was them who had done things wrong. It was them who had rejected her ideas, but by closing off her mind to the thoughts and ideas of others and using them to blame for her own lack of empathy, she was not using emotional intelligence. Mindfulness is a great remedy for this as well because it teaches you to be empathetic or to be able to put yourself into someone else's shoes and come up with solutions that not only suit self, but that will work in conjunction with others. That made her more productive, less negative and much more people friendly.

Social skills – Having tackled the rest, social skills are a walk in the park. Just like I said about my life, I had never really stopped to look beyond the surface and was incapable of reading people. When I stopped blaming people for bad things that happened in my life, it opened up a whole new realm of potential in my life and I believe it is for this reason that I am driven to write this book in the first place. It is astounding the difference in my life and I want you to have an equal opportunity to open up avenues toward happiness in your life as well. If you are now ready, take on the next chapter, but have something ready to note down your intentions, so that these actually take place rather than just being intentions that never go anywhere.

Chapter 7

21 Effective Steps to Increase EQ in Your Daily Life

In this chapter you will learn what it takes to increase your EQ and by the end of the chapter, you should be able to put these actions into motion.

1. Learning to listen

This is an important part of emotional intelligence because when you learn to listen you give other people a chance to air their views, but active listening is more than just listening to words. You can read the person in a better way when you stop and listen and will have a better handle on what makes that person tick. This also gives you a chance to think about your answers, rather than giving opinion too quickly and regretting it later.

2. Learning not to judge

This is a harder one. When you learn meditation and mindfulness it becomes easier. The reason why your emotional intelligence is lower is because you haven't yet learned to stop judging situations. People make instant judgments and can sometimes be wrong. I thought, for example, that the girl at the party didn't want to know, and wasted a lot of my time that could have been spent on getting to know her. You probably notice yourself doing things like this as well. Judgment creates negative thinking patterns. We judge people based on social expectations and may say "She is fat" or "He is not interesting" and we may even use judgment inwardly judging ourselves against set measures. It's time to realize that each individual human being has a reason for their actions and it's not your place to question them, but to accept that this is an individual right. If you want to be taken seriously in life and you want to gain more control over your emotions, this step will be a huge step in the right direction.

3. Learn to meditate

You may argue that you don't have time to meditate or that it's too complex. If you did watch the video by the neurosurgeon that was pointed to earlier in the book, you will know that her profession made her skeptical about mindfulness and meditation, but that she witnessed changes in her approach toward life that made her more compassionate and understanding of others and self. She began to see a person emerge who was more compassionate and who could use empathy in the place of apathy. It enriched her life. To meditate isn't as complex as you may imagine. All you need to do is put aside 15 minutes a day and if that means setting your alarm clock earlier, it will have been worthwhile because if you can make meditation a daily habit, you gain more from it. Sit in a hard chair with your back straight. The energy flow within the body works its way through the spine, so posture is everything. Close your eyes and make sure that you are in comfortable clothing and place your feet flat on the floor. Now, breathe in through the nostrils to the count of eight and then out to the count of ten and keep breathing in this way until your breathing forms a rhythm. When it does, start to go with that rhythm and be in this moment. That means that all of the things from the past are of no consequence and that things you have in your future are not to be thought about. Be in the breath. It's only fifteen minutes a day every morning before breakfast and the change that it will make in your life is astounding. As thoughts go through your mind, learn to dismiss them. Acknowledge them of course, because they are valid thoughts. They are simply not needed during the 15 minutes that you meditate, so let go of them. If you keep thinking, you will probably think you have failed, but it doesn't work like that. You simply kick those thoughts to one side and go on breathing and letting go of thoughts. That fifteen minutes can make a whole heap of difference to your emotional intelligence because you learn who you are. That may sound a little weird, but most people really don't spend that quiet time with themselves and don't let the subconscious mind rest enough to power them up to face the world and that's what meditation does. It allows them that freedom from thought and little by little, you find that it changes your whole perspective on life. When you know yourself better, you actually find acceptance much easier to incorporate into your life and that's amazing.

The other things that meditation will help you with is your heartbeat rate and your blood pressure and when you have finished, although you may not feel different straightaway, after practicing meditation over a prolonged period of time, you will find that you are able to concentrate m0re and that you don't let your emotions rule the roost. Instead, you have a clearer mind and are able to make decisions without the brain fog that you may have experienced in the past.

4. Learn to appreciate the moment

This is what mindfulness is all about. For example, how often do you eat your food without even noticing the taste or chewing the food correctly? What does that have to do with emotional intelligence? Well, the fact is that you are able to digest your food better and will not suffer from many of the ailments that are irritating, such as gut ache or even constipation. The stomach is a huge part of you and treating it well will help you to think more positive thoughts. You will also be able to use mindfulness to step into the moment whenever you are faced with things that are difficult for your emotions to handle. What you are doing is turning negative thought patterns into patterns that look at the moment that you are in. Instead of walking through a park thinking about the argument you had with your boss, you replace those thoughts with observations of what's happening right now. For example, you will see the plants and the seasons. You will notice things that perhaps you didn't notice before because you are being mindful of the walk and the place that you are visiting. Bringing your mind into the present moment is a way to change the habits of a lifetime. You can cull those negative thoughts and replace them with very positive ones, which will change your outlook toward life entirely. Mindfulness also slows down the process of the emotional responses that you have to live so that you are able to observe problems and cut out judgment of people and situations. Emotionally intelligent people are more versatile for a very good reason. They cut out all of the unnecessary judgment that others experience and free their minds of negativity by seeing all of the good things instead of the bad things. They also learn to drop judgment and can accept life more readily, making them less likely to make emotional mistakes. If there are mindfulness classes near you, then do take them because mindfulness helps to make you a much more compassionate person and more compassionate even toward yourself. You forgive things that happen and accept the bad with the good, but don't allow it to hold you back from thinking about positive solutions. You use all of your senses more and are able to distinguish the aromas of the world, the sights that you see and the emotional high that you get from opening your eyes and your senses to the world around you, taking any negative judgment out of the picture. This takes practice as we have already explained the amount of negative reactions people have to events that take place in their lives. Think of mindfulness as a stepping stone toward liberation from negative thinking patterns and you will start to enjoy your life more. For example, stop when you are eating and taste every texture and taste by chewing your food and concentrating on eating. Be aware of people around you and of the good things in the world, rather than letting your mind become myopic and negative thinking. Mindfulness also helps you to know yourself better and to better relate to the world around you, so will benefit you in so many different ways, including upping your ability to use emotional intelligence.

5. Learn to prioritize

The idea of prioritizing is to help you to overcome the potential of becoming emotionally overwhelmed by life. The problem is that you only have a set amount of hours in any day. If you try to fit everything into that time willy-nilly, you get to the stage where your emotions stop you from actually getting anything done at all. Thus, you need to be able to control that by knowing which tasks you need to do first and which can wait for another time. When you learn to prioritize you also have your head screwed on the right way and know that low priority jobs don't really matter that much in the order of things.

6. Turn off negative influence

When you look at people's Facebook pages, what you see is not a real world. Instead, you see what people want you to see. From drama queens all the way through to those who make you feel bad about yourself; they are all lined up ready to play with your emotions. It's time to learn when to cut off social media and it may even be a good idea to make Facebook a real place where the only friends you have are positive influences in your life. That way, you don't get emotionally sidetracked by stories that may or may not be real. So many people are putting themselves on display on these social media sites and what you see may not actually be what you think you see. Pictures get retouched, and you can even make yourself look slimmer by adjusting the photographs. Stop measuring yourself by these standards and start to be real about your life.

7. Learn to delegate and share

How does this help you? It helps you in your observation of others and helps to meet their needs to belong, instead of trying to inflate your worth and living with the emotional burden of doing so. Sharing your work with those who are around you shows a higher level of emotional intelligence. If you get stuck on something, ask someone who knows so that you will not be stuck next time. There are always people in the world who know more than you do about one particular aspect of your work, so don't feel that it demeans who you are. If you don't ask, this shows you to be lacking in understanding and unable to work with other people and you will never be chosen as potential promotion material.

8. Minimize

What does this mean? Madelaine used to put a great deal of value on the things that she owned. It was always a case of one-upmanship. She had learned this awful trait during high school, but as she got older, she suddenly found herself questioning her motives. Did anyone really care if her car was better than that of the neighbor? What about her home? Was it providing her with the comfort and peace that she was seeking? The fact was that it cost a lot of time to keep up with everyone else and many of the things she had purchased to impress others cost her dearly and were little used. When she stumbled upon the idea of minimalism, she had always thought that this meant some kind of deprivation, but following trends, she decided to give it a go. When you get rid of the clutter of things in your life, you simplify your life and find that your emotional levels are easier to handle. You are using emotional intelligence to understand that things don't buy happiness, but that this is something that should come from inside you, rather than be reflected by the number of things you own. As she decluttered her life, she found that she made more friends and that these were friends who accepted her for who she was. She also found that she liked herself more because she wasn't trying to compete and was happier with who she was. When you take away all of this bias from your life, you have room to be emotionally intelligent and to use your time in a better way, taking positive moves when it comes to sharing your time with others.

9. Exercise and fresh air

You may think this doesn't matter much when it comes to emotional intelligence, but you would be wrong. Even if all of the exercise that you get is a walk in the park every evening with the dog, it's a big step in the right direction. Why? Being in a natural environment helps you to think positively and to surround yourself with positive things. You notice the changes of the seasons, and the walk is also energizing your body and mind at the same time. People who do exercise frequently suffer less from emotional lows and are able to use that additional energy in a positive way. Erick never went walking. By the time he came home from the office, he was too tired, or that's the way he saw it. However, when they got a dog, he found that the walk in the evenings actually slowed his mind down so that he had more energy to use on the time that he did spend with his family and that this walking reduced his level of emotional strain, thus increasing his emotional intelligence and being able to relate more to people around him.

10. Minimizing Negative influences

This was a no brainer for Eleanor although she didn't see it at first. She surrounded herself with people who were either jealous of her or who used her. She allowed herself to be used and this had an impact on her self-esteem. She noticed one day that she wasn't coping well with being on her own, and thus didn't mind being used as a doormat because that was better than nothing. However, when she examined the relationships that she had in her life, she found that there were positive relationships as well as negative ones and that more and more she was spending time with people who made her feel negative. Stopping that spiral, she decided that unless people made her feel good about being herself, she had no room for them in her life. She cut down on the negative influences and became much more positive and proactive. This upped her self-esteem and also helped her to use her emotional intelligence to make her life a happier place to be.

11. Journaling and positivity

You may think that life is not offering you much, but how often have you tried to write down the positive things that you have to be grateful for? The chances are that these things happen without even being acknowledged. When you sit to eat your dinner, do you think of those who never have food to sit down to? What about when you wake up in the morning in a warm bed? Do you think of people who don't have that luxury? The problem is that we tend to err on the side of negative thought. No matter what you have, you may be yearning more without actually appreciating what you have. When you diary your gratitude toward life, you turn negative thought patterns into positive ones. If you ever watched the movie "Pollyanna", the main character was a little crippled girl. Her idea in life to overcome her handicaps was to see a positive light in every situation, and it affected all of the people around her. That's nothing new, but if you don't feel gratitude for those things that are right in your life, how will you ever be able to use emotional intelligence to pay it forward?

12. Relaxation

Often people do not take enough time to relax. This may mean that their minds are working overtime and that they are unable to see beyond how busy they are. Relaxation classes help and if you don't have time for classes, at least do a body scan when you find that your mind is overactive. This helps you to sleep and emotionally intelligent people know that the body needs time to sleep and relax so that all of the hormones that circulate in the body are able to do their healing. Lie down on a bed and lie on your back. It's best to do this in an atmosphere that is darkened, so close the drapes. You need one pillow only so that your airways are freed up. Close your eyes, breathe in through your nostrils and as you do so, start by thinking of your toes. Wiggle them and then relax them feeling them get heavier. You work your way up your body thinking of parts of your body and then tensing them and relaxing them until you are completely relaxed. Bear in mind that this will lower your blood pressure and heartbeat so don't try getting up straight away afterward. If you find that thoughts come into your mind, go back to your toes and concentrate on what you are doing. How does this help emotional intelligence? If your body and mind are too stressed, you tend to make snap judgments without really being able to digest what is happening. If you are rested, you are able to give more to your life and receive so much more in return. Your mental anguish is lowered, meaning that you are less responsive to negative emotions.

13. Eating healthy foods

Emotionally intelligent people usually eat the right kinds of foods. This is important because the body functions in a certain way given the fuel that it is fed. If you insist on eating snacks and packet foods, your body isn't getting the goodness it needs and chances are that you are overweight. This impedes your ability to love yourself and you may have self-esteem issues. Eating healthily will help you to overcome these issues.

14. Volunteerism

This is a very important change in your life because it helps you to boost your own self-esteem and stop relying upon others to boost it. If you are one of those people who is always seeking approval or validation from others, you need to learn that self-validation is much more important. Value yourself. Volunteer to help someone without any strings attached. Jennifer was always doing things to gain approval from others and when she didn't get that validation, she felt that she was not important enough. By finding a job at weekends at the local dog shelter, she found a great joy in giving her time to help out with feeding the dogs and exercising them and didn't need anyone to validate her. She was doing something for no thanks, as were the other volunteers, but it made her feel that she had value. That improved her self-esteem and an improvement in self-esteem equals the ability to control emotions and observe them so that you are more capable of upping your emotional intelligence in the process.

15. Observation

This helps you considerably to let go of pre-existing ideas. You may find that you are influenced by society into laying judgment on certain types of people. This exercise helps to show you how false those judgments are. Go to a mall and observe people. Write down the different types of people and then look to see what behavior someone exhibits that makes them:

- *Confident*

- *Attractive*

- *Friendly*

- *Positive*

Then contrast that with people who give off negative vibes. Write down the behaviors that give them negative vibes. You are learning about the way in which total strangers behave, but you are doing more than that. You are also giving yourself a chance to change. You are also giving yourself a chance to change your approach to life by taking on those traits that give the impression of confidence, friendliness and positivity instead of any negative traits that are immediately given away by your posture.

16. Body Language

In the last exercise you looked at basic body energy. Now I want you to observe even closer. This could be with friends or family members to recognize things that are given across by negative thought processes. Use a mirror and examine your own body language. This helps to make you more emotionally intelligent because you are beginning to notice:

- *Eye movements*

- *The movement of the lips*

- *The sincerity of the smile*
- *The sarcasm*
- *The wit*
- *Mockery*

If you are able to read people in a better way, this helps you to interact with them better because you are aware of their weaknesses and strengths and are able to take these into account. Anthony used this when he was interviewing people for a job. Instead of basing the interviews on academic achievement, he based them on emotional response to questions and used his emotional intelligence to give him the instinct to use wisdom when choosing the right candidate. Understanding body language also enables you to gauge when it's the right time to make an approach or to suggest new things and with that knowledge, you become much more capable of success in your life and will know whether people around you are genuine or not.

17. Improved social awareness

This is achieved by being more interactive with the world around you and the easiest way to demonstrate this is for you to walk down the street with your head held high and smile when you pass people. It sounds like a kid's game or something that won't make much difference to your world, but it's amazing the difference it makes. When you approach the world with your head down and a grimace on your face, you add no joy either to your life or to the lives of people around you. By being more socially aware and taking in what's happening in your life rather than simply walking through life with no social awareness, you open yourself to possibility and use more emotional intelligence because you will find the world reacts with you in a more positive way as well.

18. Be aware of positive behavior

You may find this a very strange thing to say, but if you are not aware of the positive things that are happening around you, you lack empathy. The girl who brings you a cup of coffee daily does so because it's her job. It's a lowly job and not the best job in the world to have but let's face it, someone has to do it. Similarly, do you think that the road sweeper likes what he does? What about the office cleaner? Each of these people is equal to you as a human being and merits positive response to the small tasks that they do. In Buddhism, you are taught to do things or comport yourself in a manner that encourages others in their lives and helps to make them happier. Although you may not appreciate having to do this until you do, you are unable to really embrace empathy in your life and that's important. There's nothing wrong with thanking the girl for the coffee and showing appreciation for the small gestures made by people around you to make your world a better place. Empathy doesn't come from not observing. It doesn't come from ignoring that everyone else's world turns in the same way that yours does. It comes from understanding that everyone is playing a small part in a bigger picture.

19. Getting close up with nature

This is something that we all need to do more of. We don't scale the hills to look across the mountains that often. But if you live in a region where there is scenery that is awe inspiring or know somewhere like that, take advantage of it to help you to understand humility. It could be a beach at sunset or sunrise, but it will be somewhere that fills you with hope and gratitude and that actually makes you feel small. Why would you want to feel small? When I visited the Himalayas, I understood the concept of this totally for the first time in my life. It doesn't matter what your religious affiliation is. What matters is that you are aware that you have a spirit within you that is capable of being spiritual. This is the part of us that is the central core to our existence and you get pretty close to understanding it when you meditate daily, but never as quickly as you do when faced by the beauty of nature. Standing on the top of my favorite hill, I am reminded about how small I am in the order of things, and that increases your emotional awareness and your ability to use emotional intelligence to see in front of you what's real and what's not real. The fact that the world is made up of small elements and that the beauty depends upon even the smallest grain of sand helps you to feel something inside that allows you to experience humility. When you start at this base level, everything that you feel in life is heightened and you can share this through using emotional intelligence with your relationships, your reactions to people and your ability to take on even the smallest of tasks. It improves who you are and the scene that you observe helps to increase your gratitude.

20. Learning about emotions

It helps you considerably to learn about positive emotions. Learn by observation of yourself. Learn what makes you angry and why. Learn what makes you feel negative feelings and examine why these happen. When you are able to do that and draw it out onto a piece of paper, then apply the fact that you are stepping away from judgment. Mindfulness will help you to do this, but you first need to examine what it is that makes you emotionally stunted. Each bias that you have and each prejudice that you experience stunts your emotional growth, so if you can journal what they are and then work on eliminating them from your life, you are in a better position to increase your emotional intelligence. Let me demonstrate this. Geoff was always made to feel small when he was with his family. This was something he kept feeling most of his life until the day his father died and the family gathered to say goodbye to him. He had spent most of his life being jealous of his sister, who seemed to have a natural talent in passing exams and showing the perfect example and his father had reminded him of this all of his life. When he spoke to her, he later examined the conversation. Not only was she made totally miserable by her father using her as the measurement of goodness, but it had stunted her enjoyment of life. She felt negative toward her brother because he had all of the freedom she had never had the luxury to experience. Much of the time, our biases and our prejudices are ill founded. In their later lives, Geoff and his sister were able to make peace with each other and actually enjoyed each other's company, both now understanding how wrong their perceptions had been all of their lives. Using emotional intelligence to examine your biases helps you to overcome them. Taking judgment out of your life also helps you to examine things as they are, rather than how you perceive them to be, as often what we perceive is one pointed and myopic. Your emotional intelligence takes a huge boost when you drop judgment and start living your life according to your own happiness levels, rather than being an underdog or trying to live your life in a superior way to impress people. When you cut out the emotional factor from the way you approach life and simply enjoy it for what it is in this moment, it becomes a lot more giving and you become more valuable as a human being.

21. Learning to let go

I left this until last for a very good reason. It's one of the most difficult hurdles to overcome when you are trying to improve your emotional intelligence. Letting go means forgiving yourself for your mistakes and learning by them. It also means letting go of blame. Blame is only a part of your life because you allow it to be and most people don't intentionally cause harm. Blame is counter-productive and instead of helping your emotional intelligence, actually stops it in its tracks. Write down all of the things you feel that you need to forgive yourself and others for. Then actively take one at a time and let go of the problem by addressing it and forgiving those involved so that you are able to feel the weight of that problem dissipate. When you do this, you will find that the load in your life becomes much lighter. "How can I forgive someone who does this?" asks one person. "How can I forgive that kind of behavior?" asks another. The fact is that if someone's behavior made you feel that you could never forgive them, they have won. They have defeated you. They are taking your emotional intelligence and screwing it into a ball so tight, you can't get out of it. You blame them. You blame someone else, but in fact when you are able to forgive and move on, your emotional intelligence takes a huge boost and you become more compassionate, both with yourself and with others. We can never really know what makes people do the things that they do. Some of the biggest mistakes of our lives may have been initially caused by others, but if we make the mistake of letting those mistakes break us, then we are as guilty as the offender because we go forward with a broken spirit and a broken life. That's why letting go is the most important thing that you can do, in order to take back control of your emotional intelligence.

Over the course of this chapter, there was a lot of activity and it won't all happen at once. You need to take one of the standpoints at a time and work on that until you are satisfied that it has made a difference in your life. Then move on to the next standpoint and work that into your life. It doesn't have to take forever and if you indeed learn to incorporate mindfulness and meditation into your life, then forgiveness and the ability to listen to your body and your instincts will also improve. Your emotional growth depends upon it and your emotional intelligence will improve with each step that you take toward that eventual goal of happiness and success.

Conclusion

I am very glad that you got this far with the book because that means that you have a better idea about what emotional intelligence is all about. You also have the tools to use it to improve your life. It took me a long time to realize and appreciate that I control how happy and successful my life is. In fact, I would say it took too long, considering that I could have used that emotional intelligence earlier in my life and had more of this happiness that I experience now every day from the moment that I wake up. Life offers us a series of experiences. Some see that cup overflowing while others are lucky to scrape the bottom of the cup, but it's not because there's nothing in the cup to enjoy. It's because they don't have the foresight to actually realize how full that cup really is.

The next time that you look at yourself in the mirror look at your eyes. They tell you a lot about your happiness level. Do they smile? Do they look skeptical? Do they look suspicious of life? Now smile and look at how that smile radiates across your face. However, realize that unless it's a genuine smile, it won't go near the wrinkles under your eyes and you won't feel that energy that true happiness brings into your life. Emotional intelligence is a shared thing. It's the way you interact to the world around you and how you receive the messages that form part of what your life becomes.

You will have learned from the book how to change your view toward the things that happen in your life, to learn by them and to help all the bad things that happen to make you grow emotionally. No one will pretend that it's easy, but the stronger you make yourself now when things are going relatively well, the easier you will find the road when bad things happen. Emotional intelligence covers so many areas of your life as I have explained in the chapters of this book and if this makes a difference to the lives of only a few readers, it will have been worth the journey.

Don't expect to "get it" straight away. We have the ability to grow our emotional intelligence, but it takes time for this to happen. However, if you really do want it to happen, nothing should stop you now that you know the route that takes you there. I have given you a lot of food for thought and a lot of evidence from professionals in the field of neuroscience and psychology and all of this points to the fact that EQ can be changed, but IQ is something you were born with. With more and more employers understanding the difference, watch out for those emotional based questions at interview because they will certainly trip up those who are not emotionally aware. Those who are will win the day because it takes more than brains to become successful. Brains and emotional intelligence will be the perfect combination to help you in all areas of your life including friendships, relationships and work oriented contact with other people, as well as the ability to enjoy your singularity as an individual.

I leave you with a quotation from Daniel Goleman 0n emotional intelligence which should make you want to turn back the pages of this book and start putting all of the tips and strategies into action in your life:

"What really matters for success, character, happiness and lifelong achievements is a definite set of emotional skills – your EQ — not just purely cognitive abilities that are measured by conventional IQ tests." — *Daniel Goleman*

Finally, if you enjoyed this book, then I'd like to ask you for a favor, would you be kind enough to leave a review for this book on Amazon? It'd be greatly appreciated!

Thank you and good luck!

Resources

https://www.scientificamerican.com/article/feeling-our-emotions/

https://www.bbc.com/news/world-us-canada-12661646

https://www.inc.com/marcel-schwantes/how-do-you-know-a-job-candidate-has-true-emotional.html

50053679R00046

Made in the USA
Middletown, DE
22 June 2019